Learning From The Ants

Learning From The Ants

"Go to the ant...consider her ways, and be wise"
[Proverbs 6:6]

Anthony Adefarakan

GLOEM, CANADA

CONTENTS

Preface 1

1st Law 3

2nd Law 5

3rd Law 7

4th Law 9

5th Law 11

6th Law 13

7th Law 15

8th Law 17

9th Law 19

10th Law 21

11th Law 23

12th Law 25

CONTENTS

| Become a Financial Partner with Jesus   27

| About the Author   29

Preface

King Solomon was a very wise man during his time because God gave him wisdom and exceedingly great understanding, and largeness of heart like the sand on the seashore (1Kings 4:29).

He was further described according to verse 33 of 1 Kings 4 (TLB) as a great naturalist, with interest in animals, birds, snakes, fish and trees – from the great cedars of Lebanon down to the tiny hyssop which grows in cracks in the wall. Little wonder he was able to say with all confidence in Proverbs 6:6 that considering the ways of ants is capable of making one wise. He must have learnt certain doses of wisdom from them.

With this wise man's recommendation in mind, I became inquisitive as to what lessons could be learnt from the ants. And fortunately for me, I was able to discover some of them.

On the 26th of October, 2009 – at about 3:45pm, I was in my old house in Nigeria relaxing with some cookies when my attention suddenly got drawn to a scene taking place on my carpet. A crumb of the biscuit had fallen to the ground and certain ants were observed taking their food into the store –a tiny hole in the wall. In their attempt to take my biscuit crumb, certain laws capable of making one wise were revealed to me, which constitute the content of this book.

I strongly believe that as you take your time to not only read these laws but also thoroughly digest them with readiness to apply them to your life, in no time you also will be referred to as wise.

Now let's learn from the ants.

Anthony Adefarakan.

1st Law

The Law of Attempt

The law states that *"You never get to know what you are capable or not capable of doing until you make an attempt. That is, your capability remains unknown until you've tried"*.

This was demonstrated by an ant which came to where the biscuit crumb fell (as narrated in the introduction). Despite the bigness of the crumb compared to its size, it was not intimidated; it still tried to carry it, although after trying and turning it for a while it gave up because it was too big for it. But the fact remains that it first attempted carrying it.

<u>Lessons:</u>

Quite a number of people tend to easily conclude that certain tasks are impossible due to the way they appear; and as a result refuse to even make an attempt. This mindset is a killer of destiny; and the cure is the correct application of this law.

It has been said that taking any action at all is far better than inaction. If David had listened to the discouraging words of his brother and even King Saul in 1 Samuel 17:28 & 33, he wouldn't have been recorded in history as the one who killed Goliath. Goliath was undoubtedly a giant, but David though being a youth was not intimidated by his size and armors. He made an attempt to kill him; and before that day was over, Goliath was dead. As a matter of fact, he beheaded him with his (Goliath's) own sword.

People who dare to make attempts are always faced with two probable outcomes – victory or defeat/gain or loss; but they never allow the fear of the negative to prevent them from experiencing the joy the positive action could also bring. They are simply unstoppable. Everything is possible to those who dare to try.

Don't be trapped in the paralysis of analysis. Too much analyses usually lead to inaction. Learn to "launch into the deep"; you never can tell what you are capable of doing until you have tried.

Now go ahead and attempt what you have always feared. It could actually yield positive results.

2nd Law

The Law of Support

The law states that *"No finger forms a fist without the cooperation of other fingers"*.

The moment the other ants saw that particular ant couldn't carry the biscuit crumb, they came around and surrounded it, making all efforts to carry it. Although, they couldn't make further progress after moving it for few seconds. All the same, they supported that ant.

Lessons:

To support means to assist or give a helping hand; and it is a very important lesson from the ants. This law is mostly applied by mature people who don't destructively criticize others' attempt at succeeding in one thing or the other but rather encourage them in any way they feel they can be supported.

Rendering support to other people is actually a way of becoming part of their success story. This support as it applies to us could be in terms of money, time, encouragement, attention, pieces of advice etc.

Supporting others to succeed is a lifestyle everyone with the mind of succeeding must cultivate. You can't help someone to succeed and remain a failure. For instance as a minister in a church, supporting your Pastor to achieve his goals will not only make the Pastor successful but also make you a minister in a successful church. When you help someone to achieve a feat, you naturally become part of their success story – which is highly rewarding.

If the ants could exhibit this, you too can. Become the assistance somebody needs to succeed; your contribution, however little, may be just what is needed. That is the way of the ants.

3rd Law

The Law of Unity

The law states that *"Any task approached with the 'our' attitude as against the 'my' or 'its' attitude would surely result in success"*.

It was observed that the other ants left their individual pursuits and turned that ant's goal to theirs as well. This they did by coming around not just to support but also to ensure the ant's vision (which they saw as theirs too) came to pass.

Lessons:

Unity is a very strong force in accomplishing any group task. This can be in form of unity of purpose, unity of approach, unity of attention, unity of time frame, unity of effort etc.

Practically nothing is impossible to people who operate in unity – that is, people who work with the 'our' attitude. Even God in Genesis 11:6 confessed that He couldn't do anything to stop the people from building the tower of Babel they had purposed to build. He had to resolve to breaking their cord of unity through disorganizing their language in order to stop them. They were unable to continue with the project only because they couldn't understand one another.

The ants knew they all had one purpose - which was to gather in as much food as possible into the store before the gathering season was over. As a result of this unity of purpose, they worked hand-in-hand. And this tells us something straight away; in every organization we find ourselves, the visions and goals of the organization must become ours too. We are to run with the vision with all sense of purpose. We shouldn't be insisting on having things done our own way or doing what we feel is right for us. There should always be a consensus.

Everyone must work to ensure the vision of the organization comes to pass. There shouldn't be any transgressor or traitor. The very consciousness of unity must be fully imprinted on everyone's mental screen. That's the way to unstoppable progress and collective achievement.

4th Law

The Law of Bits

The law states that *"Whatever task cannot be accomplished as a whole can surely be accomplished in bits and pieces"*.

As I watched, some of the gathered ants climbed the crumb and started tearing it down into tiny pieces; tiny enough for an average ant to carry without any assistance. The biscuit crumb was being disintegrated by some of the ants while the others kept coming and taking the food into their store in bits. They did it one bit at a time.

Lessons:

Many tasks have been left undone simply because they appear so cumbersome.

If a farmer looks up and sees the size of the land he has to clear before planting his crops, he may be discouraged. But if he takes his cutlass and starts clearing from a particular portion of the land, he will in no time finish the task. In that case, he would have engaged the law of bits.

Some students don't write or type notes because of the number of pages they have to copy. But if only they can forget about the number of pages and just start writing or typing from somewhere, in no time, they would have finished the whole task.

This is a very wonderful wisdom from the ants. The biscuit crumb which they could not carry as a whole they carried in bits.

This teaches us that we must never admit failure whenever we are faced with insurmountable tasks. All we need do is start from somewhere; and before we know it, it would have been accomplished.

A big ocean is a product of little drops of water, and it takes 3,600 rounds of continuous ticking for a clock to achieve one hour. Start that big task now, and you will be glad you did.

5th Law

The Law of Tenacity

The law states that *"Persistence is the key to overcome resistance"*.

The ants dismantling the crumb kept at it tenaciously despite the difficulty they experienced in doing it. They remained there for over one hour (3:45 – 4:53pm); ensuring the whole crumb was dismantled for easy carriage into the store.

Lessons:

Every champion is a fighter; and they must have won at least a battle or a fight to be declared and addressed as such. Difficulties and oppositions are inevitable in any project worth achieving. There must be at least a form of resistance in the execution of such projects. However, it is the reaction of the one involved that determines either the success or the failure of the project.

Tenacity implies holding on firmly to a thing – a course of action, a principle, an idea, or anything worth achieving - regardless of any present contrary force or opinion. This is what it means to persist – to hold on, to keep at something until it is achieved. The ants exhibited this.

One hour is a long period for common tiny ants to be engaged in a single task without quitting. They must have been bored, their fragile appendages must have been aching and it surely must have appeared as if the task was not going to be completed; but they kept at it all the same.

The implication of this is that once we have determined to execute a task, we must be ready to disregard every form of distraction, resistance or problem that may arise in the course of the execution and hold on tenaciously until the task is completed. In fact if you must know, it is the amount or level of opposition and resistance your project attracts that validates the worth of the project.

Without resistance, the project may not be a worthwhile one in the first place.

6th Law

The Law of Retrial

The law states that *"Falling isn't as bad as accepting it as a state. That is, you may -fall; but you should never remain on the ground"*.

While one of the ants was on its way to the store with a piece of the biscuit crumb, the piece fell; and being unable to pick it up by itself, the ant went back to the site and picked another one it was able to carry without delay or any form of self-pity.

Soon after, another ant that was returning to the site for a piece saw the fallen piece and being strong enough to carry it, it simply used its initiative (without asking questions) and carried it to the store before continuing its own exercise. The two ants knew what to do without receiving any instructions from anyone.

Lessons:

Failure is never a state; it's only an event. That is, it's just an occurrence.

Simply because your plans did not work out this time doesn't mean it can never work out. And just because you fell in the journey of life doesn't mean you cannot rise again. The Bible says even your righteousness is not an immunity against falling; but the good news is that your Samson's hair can grow again [Proverbs 24:16, Judges 16:22].

The law of retrial is what saw Thomas Edison through. He failed 9,999 times in trying to invent an incandescent bulb; but at the $10,000^{th}$ time, he got it right. Also, Abraham Lincoln kept trying after series of losses, and he eventually became one of the greatest Presidents of the United States of America.

Always be ready to retry; you never can tell if it's the next attempt that will bring you the much anticipated success. It was said that Professor Wole Soyinka (the first African to be awarded the Noble Prize in Literature) failed in English Language 8 times at a point in his life; but today he is a globally recognized authority in that same subject just because he kept trying.

No matter how many times you've failed, 'get back to the site for another piece of crumb'.

7th Law

The Law of Concentration

The law states that *"Any task denied concentration ends up becoming a burden"*.

Some of the ants that were going about their own businesses were seen changing direction and coming to finish up the main task at hand. They didn't say things like 'that's not my business'; they stopped searching and gathered with full concentration to see the end of the biscuit crumb. They all concentrated their efforts; not even minding my torch light which I was flashing at them at the time. They were so focused.

Lessons:

Concentration is a major factor in accomplishing any given task. It channels all the energy, focus, attention, time and everything needed towards the project until it's done. Individual light rays may not be strong enough to cut through a metal, but when they concentrate as a laser beam, they become strong enough to cut through.

When for instance you decide to write a book and you actually start, the moment you deny the work the needed concentration probably by doing something else that commands your attention, the book project becomes a burden. In fact, it may get to a point when you will begin to doubt if actually planned to write the book.

Lack of concentration is seen in having many things to do but not being able to accomplish any. As trivial as tying your shoe lace appears, without concentration you might be on it for over 10 minutes. May be you are talking with someone; you will discover that you keep leaving the shoe lace to make a point. And the moment you get back to tying it, you suddenly discover there is another point to make.

Before you know it, what you could have done in less than 2 minutes would have taken more than 10 minutes to accomplish.

The only way to correct lack of concentration is to start focusing. That is, concentrating consciously.

8th Law

The Law of Moderation

The law states that *"Excessiveness is a sign of greed and indiscipline with moderation as its only cure"*.

As big and many as the pieces of the biscuit crumbs were to the ants, they didn't carry beyond their sizes. Once they noticed they couldn't carry certain pieces, they dropped them for the ones they could carry. As their sizes vary, so are their abilities and so were the pieces each one carried.

Lessons:

Moderation is a very great virtue. It shows maturity and good character outlook. As a matter of fact, it can successfully act as a synonym to perfection. Moderation as it applies to us has application in every aspect of our lives – in talking, dressing, sleeping, eating, buying, selling, business, relationships etc. It's such an admirable virtue.

To be moderate means not being excessive. Some of us eat until we develop constipation as a result of indigestion simply because the food is so much available to us. At other times, we talk and talk until we begin to reveal personal secrets unconsciously simply because we fail to establish 'stops'.

The Bible says we should let our moderation be known unto all men (Philippians 4:5). Everyone who desires to be great in life must take conscious steps to become moderate in all things; such that when talking, they know when to stop; when eating, they know when to stop and when sleeping, they know when to get up. In fact, anyone who follows the timing of events as recorded in Ecclesiastes 3:1-8 will be moderate and even perfect in all they do.

Moderation however doesn't occur naturally; it must be cultivated through discipline. And if the ants could practice it, you too can.

9th Law

The Law of Completion

The law states that *"No task or assignment is completed until it ceases to exist as a task; not when abandoned or postponed"*.

The ants practiced the principle that says whatever has a beginning must surely have an end. They kept coming and the ones with the crumb kept dismantling it, ensuring all was taken in. It took them over an hour, but they completed it. Not even the smallest piece was left on site.

Lessons:

The Word of God says the end of a thing is better than the beginning thereof (Ecclesiastes 7:8a). No athlete has ever received a prize for starting a race; it's always awarded at the end of the race. It is useless to commence a project and abandon it half way. In such case, all the efforts dissipated in commencing it amount to waste.

In starting anything in life – be it school, business, training, medication etc, you must be fully prepared to get to the end of it no matter how long it takes. An abandoned project brings shame to the executor (Luke 14:28-30). Now take a moment and think about how many projects you have abandoned due to one excuse or the other. And it has been discovered that leaving tasks uncompleted drains up the motivation and energy required to start new ones while the joy of completion supplies the motivation to take up new projects.

A project that will not be completed in my opinion should not be commenced in the first place. To have our projects completed however, we must first learn to focus on the joy that comes with completion rather than focusing on the immediate hindrances. This will release the strength needed to continue when it seems there is no way to forge ahead.

If you must apply this law, then you will have to revisit your abandoned projects and get them completed. That's the way of the ants the Bible encourages you to consider (Proverbs 6:6).

10th Law

The Law of Speed

The law states that *"In rewarding success, speed of accomplishment constitutes a main factor as it determines how many of such success can be recorded"*.

The ants were very time conscious. The moment they ascertained they could carry a particular piece they sped off; coming back for more almost immediately. They didn't wait to talk on the road; it was as though they had a time frame of accomplishment in mind.

Lessons:

Time is a very impatient friend. As nice as it appears to be, it waits for no one. This was the underlying principle those ants operated with. They were practically rushing as if someone was about to ring the time-up bell. Many people in life would have been recorded as successful if only they valued time. They would have become celebrities but for the poor attitude they had towards time.

As you go on in this journey of life, you must learn to operate within time-frames. Don't set endless or timeless goals. Let your plans be time bound. That's the way to succeed.

Achieving success is not as important as achieving it within the set time-frame. This is what determines how many of such success can be recorded. Henceforth, decide on what you want to achieve within a period of time and set forth into action (like the ants). Let the time set dictate your momentum; and before you know it, you will see yourself recording success right in time. But if you fail to set a time-frame or deadline, you will most likely waste some time. And peradventure you eventually hit the success, it would be out of time. Thus, speed of accomplishment is one of the ingredients that makes success sweet.

11th Law

The Law of Endurance

The law states that *"Good and lasting success is often baked in the oven of endurance"*.

If it's worth achieving, then it's worth enduring. The ants moved freely when they were light; but the moment they carried their portions, movement became a more careful exercise. They endured the inconvenience from site to the store without complaint. That's endurance.

Lessons:

Endurance actually means persevering towards the achievement of a purpose. Without an end in view, endurance simply becomes an exercise in futility. To endure, you must have something you are willing to achieve.

In the case of the ants, they had to endure because it is the food they gather in summer that will sustain them throughout winter. So, they knew they were going to celebrate later if only they could endure for a while.

In this life, good and glorious things don't come cheaply. Even Jesus Christ the Son of God had to endure the cross - despising the shame (Hebrews 12:2). He saw it as a temporary pain He needed to go through before He could sit at the right Hand of the Father, far above principalities and powers.

Now everyone calls on His Name for salvation, redemption, healing, deliverance, protection, provision etc. But for all these to happen through His Name, He had to pay the price of endurance with His own very blood. He knew what He was doing; He said if He laid down

His life, He would pick it up again. So, He chose to endure the entire process.

Hardly will anyone record a good and lasting success without engaging the principle of endurance; this is because the road isn't always a smooth one.

But then, remember this: 'if it's worth achieving, it's worth enduring'.

12th Law

The Law of Discipline

The law states that *"The lack of self-restraint is a sure recipe for self-destruction"*.

The ants were observed to be highly disciplined. Though the biscuit crumbs they were carrying were edible, and the position of carriage was close to their mouths, yet they delivered faithfully to the store. They exercised great restraint by not eating what was meant to be stored; despite not being monitored or supervised. They were purpose oriented and as such exhibited delayed gratification. Ants are indeed wise.

Lessons:

Discipline is all about showing restraint despite all contrary pressures. It is a principle that cuts across every sphere of a man's life – be it spiritual, financial, marital, physical, academics etc. A disciplined person does not operate without boundaries. They have established boundaries.

For instance, a man who has determined never to borrow money will hold on to his stand no matter what happens. That's discipline. It's a very clear sign of integrity.

A disciplined man will not eat when he is not hungry; he will not speak when there's nothing to say; he will not buy things he doesn't need and he will not make a promise he knows he can't keep.

Discipline was demonstrated by Daniel in the Book of Daniel, chapter one and verse eight. He stood his ground by not defiling himself with the king's meat.

Instant gratification has become a great problem these days; everyone wants everything, now. And that's causing a lot of trouble already.

Bribery, corruption, jumping queues etc are all offshoots of the 'now' syndrome.

But in the case of the ants, they didn't eat what was meant to sustain them in the future; they exhibited restraint. It wasn't because the biscuit was not sweet or edible; but somehow they knew it wasn't meant to be eaten at that time.

The one virtue you need to secure your future from today's provision is discipline. Learn this from the ants.

Become a Financial Partner with Jesus

At *Global Emancipation Ministries - Calgary*, our mandate is *to liberate men through the knowledge of the Truth* and our mission statement is *creating channels through which men can encounter the Truth*
[Isaiah 61:1-3; John 8:32, 36; I Thessalonians 5:24].

Our Ministerial Activities include Rural and Urban Evangelical Outreaches, Prison Evangelism, Hospital Ministrations, Mobilization for Missions Support, Teaching of the undiluted Word of God, Scripture-Based Seminars, Discipleship, Training of Field Missionaries and Empowerment of underprivileged ones among other Field Ministerial Tasks.

If you sense the Lord is calling you to reach out to the lost by engaging in any of these activities or by assisting those involved with your resources, please feel free to join us. Let us come together as we take the Gospel of our Lord Jesus Christ to the hurting and forgotten ones.
[Mark 16:15-20].

Please join us in these kingdom projects by making your weekly, monthly, quarterly or annual donations to Global Emancipation Ministries – Calgary.

You can visit the "GIVE" section on our website, www.gloem.org, to learn about other ways to give.

For acknowledgement, please advise your donations to us by email: info@gloem.org or emancipation4souls@yahoo.com, and kindly include your details i.e. name, address, email and location. Alternatively, you can simply call +1 587 9735910 to do same.

You can also volunteer your gifts and talents in the service of the Lord through our ministerial platforms regardless of your location. To get information on how to go about this, please visit www.gloem.org and contact us via email: info@gloem.org or emancipation4souls@yahoo.com.

God bless you.

About the Author

By the special grace of God, **Anthony O. Adefarakan** is the privileged President of **Global Emancipation Ministries - Calgary (GLOEM)** with headquarters in Canada, North America and **Emancipating Truth Ministry International (ETMI)** with headquarters in Nigeria, West Africa.

The Lord called him into the field ministry in February 2008 with the mandate to liberate men through the knowledge of the Truth, and by December 2012 he was ordained and commissioned as the Pioneer Pastor – in – Charge of The Redeemed Christian Church of God, Revelation Parish, Shalom Area under Delta Province III, Nigeria where he served until 1st February 2015 when he officially handed over to a new Pastor in order to focus on his field ministry to which the Lord had earlier called him and for which the authority of the church had already prayed and released him to undertake.

On 29th September 2013, he was awarded a Post Graduate Diploma in Tent – Making Mission from the Redeemed Christian School of Missions, Nigeria (RECSOM, Asaba Campus) where he also had the privilege to train Pastors and Missionaries as a lecturer in 2017.

Since the commissioning of his field ministry in 2015 he has had the opportunity to lead his ministry officers to field ministrations in different Prisons, Hospitals, Orphanages, Rural communities, Camp settlements, Markets, Local churches among other places with great successes on all occasions – such as salvation of sinners, healing of the sick, financial empowerment of mission churches, provision of relief materials to the poor, provision of medical services to the underprivileged, baptism in the Holy Ghost, deliverance from demonic oppression, release of inmates just to mention a few - all to the glory of God Who alone is the Doer.

He is the author of other best-selling titles such as *The Law of Kinds, It's Your Size, The Immutability of God's Counsel, Surely there is an End, Life Applicable lessons from the Book of Ruth, One thing is Needful, Life Applicable Revelations from God's Word* among others.

He is happily married to Ifeoluwa A. Adefarakan and their marriage is fruitful to the glory of God.

Jesus is his Message, Freedom is the Outcome!
Isaiah 61:1-3

www.ingramcontent.com/pod-product-compliance
Lightning Source LLC
Chambersburg PA
CBHW071918070526
44583CB00016B/2040